T0080611

Pebble® Plus

Asian Animals

Orangutans

by Joanne Mattern

Consulting Editor: Gail Saunders-Smith, PhD

Content Consultant: Tanya Dewey, PhD
University of Michigan Museum of Zoology

CAPSTONE PRESS
a capstone imprint

Pebble Plus is published by Capstone Press,
1710 Roe Crest Drive, North Mankato, Minnesota 56003.
www.capstonepub.com

Copyright © 2010 by Capstone Press, a Capstone imprint. All rights reserved.
No part of this publication may be reproduced in whole or in part, or stored in a retrieval system, or transmitted in any form or by any means, electronic, mechanical, photocopying, recording, or otherwise, without written permission of the publisher. For information regarding permission, write to Capstone Press,
1710 Roe Crest Drive, North Mankato, Minnesota 56003.

Library of Congress Cataloging-in-Publication Data
Mattern, Joanne, 1963–
Orangutans / by Joanne Mattern.
p. cm. — (Pebble Plus. Asian animals)
Includes bibliographical references and index.
Summary: "Simple text and photographs present orangutans, how they look, where they live, and what they do" — Provided by publisher.
ISBN 978-1-4296-4030-5 (library binding)
ISBN 978-1-4296-4848-6 (paperback)
1. Orangutan — Juvenile literature. I. Title. II. Series.
QL737.P96M38 2010
599.88'3 — dc22 2009028650

Editorial Credits
Katy Kudela, editor; Matt Bruning, designer; Svetlana Zhurkin, media researcher; Eric Manske, production specialist

Photo Credits
Alamy: Ben Oliver, 13, Ben Queenborough, 21; Biosphoto: Cyril Ruoso, 17; Getty Images: A & J Visage, 7; iStockphoto: George Clerk, 19; Minden Pictures: Anup Shah, 5, Cyril Ruoso, 11; Newscom: Photoshot/NHPA/Andy Rouse, 15; Shutterstock: Andy Z., cover, capturefoto, 1, Marcel Suliman, 9

Note to Parents and Teachers

The Asian Animals series supports national science standards related to life science. This book describes and illustrates orangutans. The images support early readers in understanding the text. The repetition of words and phrases helps early readers learn new words. This book also introduces early readers to subject-specific vocabulary words, which are defined in the Glossary section. Early readers may need assistance to read some words and to use the Table of Contents, Glossary, Read More, Internet Sites, and Index sections of the book.

Printed in the United States 5372

Table of Contents

Living in Asia 4
Up Close!. 8
Eating and Drinking 12
Staying Safe 18

Glossary 22
Read More 23
Internet Sites 23
Index. 24

Living in Asia

Orangutans climb and swing through Asia's rain forests. As adults, these quiet apes live by themselves.

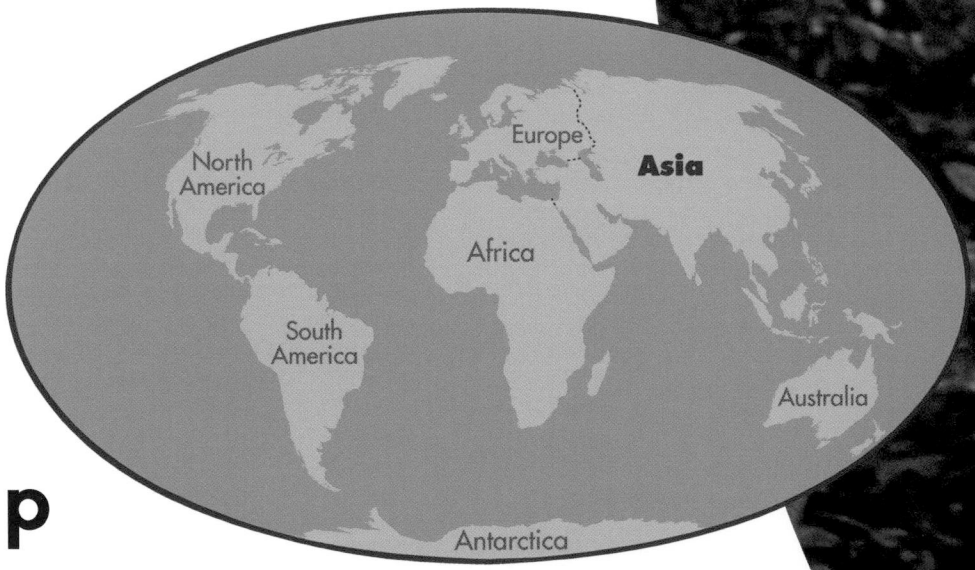

World Map

Orangutans live on the islands
of Borneo and Sumatra.
They build and sleep in
new nests each night.

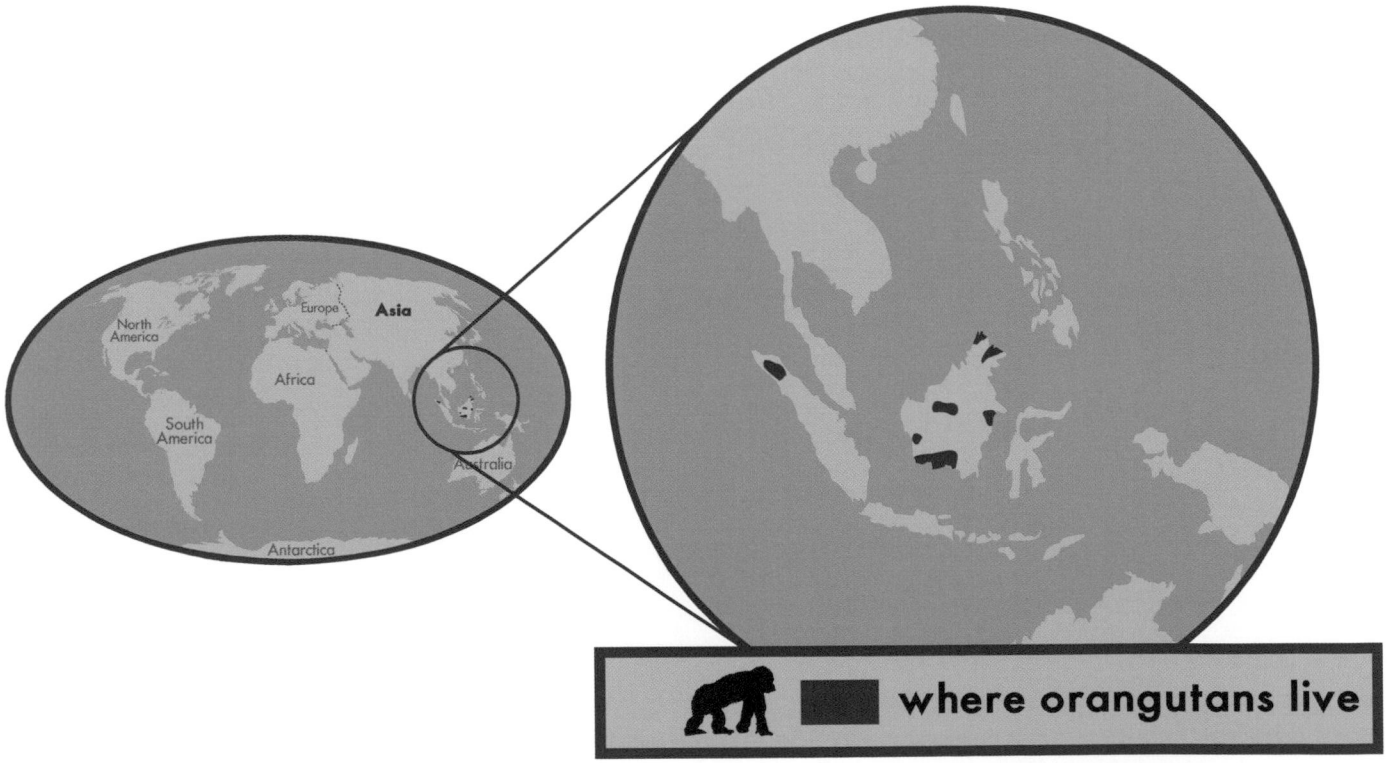

Up Close!

Orangutans have
thick, red-brown hair.
Hair covers their bodies
from head to toe.

Orangutans have long arms
to swing from tree to tree.
Their fingers and toes
grip branches and vines.

Eating and Drinking

Orangutans munch on

fruits, nuts, and plants.

They also catch insects.

Orangutans use sticks
to dig insects from tree bark.
They use rocks to smash open
fruits and nuts.

Orangutans use their hands

to scoop water.

They also drink rainwater

that collects on leaves.

Staying Safe

A mother orangutan
protects her baby.
She teaches her baby
to climb and find food.

Orangutans are endangered.
They have few places to live.
People passed laws
to protect orangutans
and their rain forest homes.

Glossary

ape — a large animal related to a monkey but with no tail; chimpanzees, gorillas, and orangutans are kinds of apes.

endangered — in danger of dying out

insect — a small animal with a hard outer shell, six legs, three body sections, and two antennae; most insects have wings.

law — a rule made by the government that must be obeyed

protect — to keep safe

rain forest — a thick area of trees where rain falls almost every day

vine — a plant with a long stem that grows along the ground or climbs on trees, fences, or other supports

Read More

Armentrout, David, and Patricia Armentrout. *Orangutans*. Amazing Apes. Vero Beach, Fla.: Rourke, 2008.

Bredeson, Carmen. *Orangutans Up Close.* Zoom in on Animals! Berkeley Heights, N.J.: Enslow Elementary, 2009.

Underwood, Deborah. *Watching Orangutans in Asia.* Wild World. Chicago: Heinemann Library, 2006.

Internet Sites

FactHound offers a safe, fun way to find Internet sites related to this book. All of the sites on FactHound have been researched by our staff.

Here's all you do:

Visit *www.facthound.com*

FactHound will fetch the best sites for you!

Index

apes, 4
arms, 10
Borneo, 6
climbing, 4, 18
colors, 8
drinking, 16
eating, 12, 14, 18
endangered, 20
fingers, 10
habitat, 4, 6, 20
hair, 8
laws, 20
nests, 6
rain forests, 4, 20
sleeping, 6
Sumatra, 6
swinging, 4, 10
toes, 10
young, 18

Word Count: 145
Grade: 1
Early-Intervention Level: 18